D0764114

Science Matters
FOSSILS

Megan Lappi

WEIGL PUBLISHERS INC.

Published by Weigl Publishers Inc.
350 5th Avenue, Suite 3304, PMB 6G
New York, NY USA 10118-0069
Web site: www.weigl.com
Copyright 2005 WEIGL PUBLISHERS INC.

Library of Congress Cataloging-in-Publication Data

Lappi, Megan.
  Fossils / Megan Lappi.
      p. cm. -- (Science matters)
  Includes index.
  ISBN 1-59036-213-6 (lib. bdg. : alk. paper) ISBN 1-59036-249-7 (softcover)
  1. Fossils--Juvenile literature. I. Title. II. Series.
  QE714.5.L357 2005
  560--dc22

                              2004004136

Printed in the United States of America
1 2 3 4 5 6 7 8 9 0 08 07 06 05 04

Project Coordinator Tina Schwartzenberger
Substantive Editor Heather C. Hudak **Copy Editor** Frances Purslow
Design Terry Paulhus **Layout** Bryan Pezzi
Photo Researcher Ellen Bryan

Photograph Credits

Every reasonable effort has been made to trace ownership and to obtain permission to reprint copyright material. The publishers would be pleased to have any errors or omissions brought to their attention so that they may be corrected in subsequent printings.

Cover: Albertosaurus from Photos.com
Bettmann/CORBIS/MAGMA: page 19; **Corel Corporation:** page 13M; **Breck Kent:** page 14; **Mary Evans Picture Library:** page 18; **Gary S. Morgan:** page 15; **Photos.com:** pages 1, 3T, 3M, 3B, 6, 8, 11, 12, 13B, 21, 22T, 22B, 23T, 23B; **J.D. Taylor:** page 17; **Tom Stack & Associates:** pages 4 (Tom & Therisa Stack), 10 (Tom & Therisa Stack), 16 (Tom & Therisa Stack); **Visuals Unlimited:** page 9 (Jeff Daly); **Roger Weller:** pages 7, 13T.

Contents

Studying Fossils

Fossils are the rocklike remains of ancient animals and plants. A fossil can be a hard part of an animal, such as a shell or a tooth. It can also be a footprint left behind in the mud. Fossils are usually found in layered rock called sedimentary rock.

The word fossil comes from the Latin word *fossilis,* which means "dug up."

■ A dragonfly that is preserved as a fossil looks exactly the same as a living dragonfly.

Fossil Facts

Fossils teach scientists about the past. They help scientists understand what Earth was like before humans lived.

- Skull fossils help scientists learn how dinosaurs heard, saw, smelled, and thought. Footprint fossils tell scientists how fast dinosaurs ran.

- A person who studies fossils for a living is called a paleontologist.

- Paleontologists study fossilized **dung** called coprolites. This helps them understand what dinosaurs ate.

- Many of the dinosaurs in museums are not really fossils. They are copies of the original fossils, made from lightweight materials.

Gone Forever

Millions of plant and animal **species** have lived on Earth during the past 3 billion years. Many of these species, such as dinosaurs, are now **extinct**. Paleontologists study fossils to learn about creatures and plants that lived in the past. Fossils tell when and how these plants and animals lived. However, fossils have not been found for many species. Scientists may never find fossils for some species.

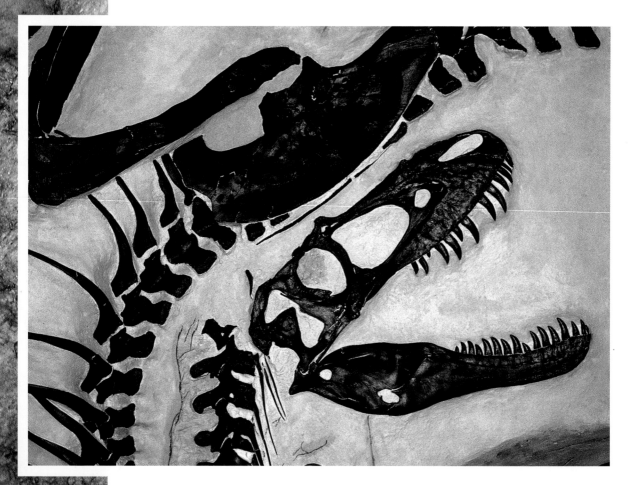

■ Fossils of the Albertosaurus, such as the one above, are rare. This dinosaur lived 74 to 76 million years ago.

A Fossil is Born

Most animals and plants do not become fossils. Many of them rot. Others dry up and blow away in the wind. Some are eaten by **scavengers**. A fossil forms

when a plant or the body of a dead animal is covered by mud. Over time, **sediment** covers the body or plant. After thousands of years, it becomes a fossil. Only a few plants and animals become fossils. Still, fossils continue to form every day. Future scientists will find the fossils that formed today.

Scientists have found many sea creature fossils. This is because sediment is usually deposited, or laid down, in the ocean.

How Fossils Form

Fossils can form in many ways. The remains of a plant or animal may be replaced by **minerals**. They may be dissolved over time so that only an **impression** remains. They may change to a different form.

Many fossils become stone. This happens when salt water enters a plant or animal's remains. Over time, the water evaporates and the remains crystallize, or harden. The plant or animal remains appear to have turned to stone. Petrified Forest National Park in Arizona has many trees that have become stone.

● Arizona's Petrified Forest National Park contains fossils that are 225 million years old.

Insects in Amber

Not all plants and animals become stone fossils. Sometimes a whole plant or animal is **preserved**. Then scientists see exactly what the plant or animal looked like when it was alive. Millions of years ago, sticky sap oozed from pine tree stems. Sometimes an insect or plant seed became stuck in the sap. Over time, the sap hardened and became another type of fossil, called amber.

Amber is yellow and looks like glass. Today, people make jewelry out of amber. Amber pieces with fossils of insects or seeds inside them are valuable.

■ Most amber is mined. Lumps weighing up to 18 pounds (8 kilograms) have been discovered.

Dinosaur Footprints

Footprints left in mud are called trace fossils. These fossils tell scientists how fast an animal moved. Trace fossils tell the animal's height and weight, too. Very large animal footprints are spaced far apart. Small animal footprints are close together. If many animal footprints are found together, scientists know that the animals lived together in herds.

The smallest dinosaur footprint found was only 1 inch (2.54 centimeters) long. The footprint was likely made by an animal about the size of a sparrow.

■ Trace fossils are more common than fossils of an entire body. One animal can leave thousands of traces behind.

Make Your Own Footprint

Have you ever thought about making your own footprint? Try the experiment below to create your very own trace fossil.

First, find a piece of clay. Place the clay on a piece of cardboard. Then, smooth and flatten the clay using a rolling pin. The clay should be about 2 inches (5.1 cm) thick. Take off your shoe and sock. Press your bare foot into the clay to make a footprint.
Now set the clay aside to harden.
After a few days, the clay will be as hard as stone. One day it will be a fossil.

Fossils Over Time

Scientists have divided Earth's history into blocks of time called eras. Different types of animals lived during each era. Fossils form in layers in the rock. Scientists can tell which eras animals lived in from the layer of rock that contains the fossils. Fossils found in upper layers are younger than fossils found in lower layers.

Precambrian Era

4.6 billion to 545 million years ago

During this time, simple life forms, such as **algae**, appeared in Earth's oceans.

4.6 billion years ago

Precambrian Era

12

Paleozoic Era

545 million to 250 million years ago

During this era, insects, fish, land plants, and the first reptiles appeared on Earth.

Mesozoic Era

250 million to 65 million years ago

During this era, dinosaurs and birds appeared. This era is also known as the "Age of Reptiles."

Cenozoic Era

65 million years ago to present

All types of **mammals**, including humans, appeared during this era. The Cenozoic Era is also called the "Age of Mammals."

545 million years ago	250 million years ago	65 million years ago
		today
Paleozoic Era	Mezozoic Era	Cenozoic Era

Dinosaur Detectives

Paleontologists study fossils to understand the types of life that were on Earth millions of years ago. Some paleontologists search for fossils. Fossils are also found by other people. Some people see part of a fossil sticking out of the ground.

Once a fossil is discovered, it is a paleontologist's job to remove the fossil from the ground. The fossil is sent to a laboratory to be studied.

● Paleontologists often work outdoors, digging for fossils.

Digging Up the Past

Digging up a fossil is difficult. Paleontologists must be careful not to damage the fossil.

First, paleontologists use small tools to clear away the material around the fossil. Then someone takes photographs and draws pictures of the site. Paleontologists study these images later.

If a fossil is surrounded by soft material, such as clay, it is wrapped in layers of cloth dipped in plaster. When the plaster sets, the fossil is turned over. Then the other side is plastered. Each fossil is labeled, so the scientists in the laboratory know what it is and where it was found.

Piecing the Puzzle Together

Once the fossilized pieces of an animal or plant are at the laboratory, paleontologists remove the plaster jackets. They use power tools to carefully remove rock from each fossil. Once all the rock is removed, the fossilized pieces are glued together.

Complete fossilized skeletons may be displayed in the museum. The pieces are very heavy, so a copy is often made using molds of the original bones. A steel framework is built, and the bones are connected together.

■ Fossils of complete skeletons are rare and valuable. Paleontologists can learn more from complete skeletons.

What Did Dinosaurs Look Like?

Paleontologists know what the skin of some dinosaurs looked like. This is because they have found fossilized impressions of their skin.

Paleontologists have no way of knowing the dinosaur's skin color. However, some scientists believe dinosaurs had good eyesight. This may mean their skin was brightly colored so other dinosaurs could see them.

Meat-eating dinosaurs may have had spots or stripes like a leopard or a tiger. Plant-eating dinosaurs may have been **camouflaged** to hide from **predators** such as *Tyrannosaurus rex*. Scientists may never know exactly how dinosaurs looked.

The Great Bone Rush

The first dinosaur bones were found in the 1820s. At first, people did not know what they had found. Soon, they realized that reptile-like creatures must have once lived on Earth. In 1842, British scientist Sir Richard Owen called these creatures *Dinausauria*, which means "terrible lizards."

In the 1870s, the "Bone Wars" began in the United States. Two men, Othniel Charles Marsh and Edward Drinker Cope, competed to find fossils. To get the fossils to museums quickly, the two men covered the fossils in plaster. This technique is still used today.

■ Sir Richard Owen was a surgeon. He studied anatomy, fossils, and dinosaurs.

A Life of Science

Barnum Brown

Barnum Brown was one of the greatest fossil hunters of the twentieth century. He was a paleontologist for 66 years. Brown traveled all over the world collecting dinosaur and mammal fossils. He was the first person to discover the bones of a fierce meat-eating dinosaur. Later, he called the dinosaur *Tyrannosaurus rex*.

Surfing Our Earth

How can I find more information about fossils?

- Libraries have many interesting books about fossils.
- Natural history museums are great places to learn about fossils.
- The Internet offers some great Web sites dedicated to fossils.

Where can I find a good reference Web site to learn more about fossils?

Encarta Homepage

www.encarta.com

- Type any fossil-related term into the search engine. Some terms to try include "dinosaur" and "paleontology."

How can I find out more about fossils, dinosaurs, and paleontology?

Strange Science

www.strangescience.net

- This Web site offers information about dinosaurs, fossils, and paleontology. It includes a time line, references for further research, and a collection of famous mistakes.

Science in Action

Looking for Fossils

Ask an adult to take you on a hike so you can look for fossils. A good place to look is along the edges of cliffs. Take a magnifying glass so you can look closely at the rock layers. Make notes about what you find. If you find something interesting, leave it behind for others to discover.

Make Your Own Fossil

It takes millions of years to make a fossil. You can begin the fossil process at home.

Fill a plastic container with dirt. Add some water to the dirt. Stir the mixture until it is thick. Now find an object, such as a shell or stick, and push it into the mud until it is completely covered. Set the mixture aside for a few days until it hardens. Now bury the hardened mixture outside. It will take a long time, but one day, this may be a fossil.

What Have You Learned?

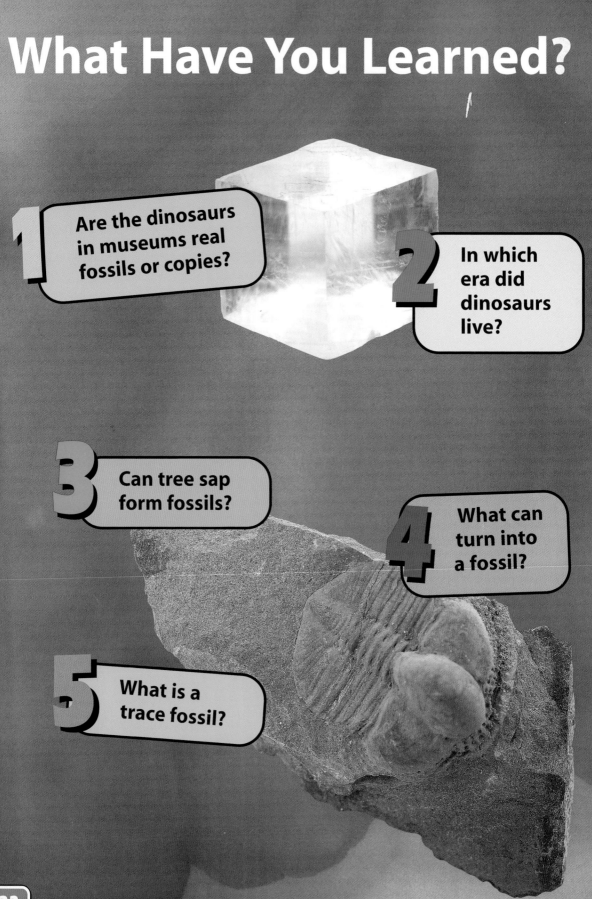

1 Are the dinosaurs in museums real fossils or copies?

2 In which era did dinosaurs live?

3 Can tree sap form fossils?

4 What can turn into a fossil?

5 What is a trace fossil?

6 When were fossils first discovered?

7 In what kind of rocks are fossils often found?

8 What can paleontologists learn by studying coprolites?

9 Which famous paleontologist discovered *Tyrannosaurus rex*?

10 What does fossil mean in Latin?

Answers: 1. The dinosaurs in museum displays are copies of fossils, made from lightweight materials. **2.** The Mesozoic Era **3.** Yes. Insects and plant seeds can be preserved as fossils in hardened tree sap called amber. **4.** Plants, animals, insects, and sea creatures can all turn into fossils. **5.** A trace fossil shows where an animal or plant lived. An example is a dinosaur footprint. **6.** Fossils were first discovered in the 1820s. **7.** sedimentary rock **8.** Coprolites tell paleontologists what an animal ate. **9.** Barnum Brown **10.** dug up

Words to Know

algae: simple living things made up of one or more cells; the basic units of living matter

camouflaged: colored so that animals blend into their surroundings

dung: animal droppings or manure

extinct: no longer alive anywhere on Earth

impression: mark left behind after pressure is applied to an object

mammals: warm-blooded animals that nurse their young

minerals: solid materials found in the natural environment

predators: animals that kill and eat other animals

preserved: something that has not changed over time

scavengers: animals that eat dead animals

sediment: material from rocks carried by water, wind, or ice, and left somewhere else

species: a group of similar animals

Index